Genius Gardening Hacks:
Tips and Fixes for the
Creative Gardener

Easy-Growing Gardening Series #10

Rosefiend Cordell

Rosefiend Publishing

Copyright © 2018 Melinda R. Cordell

ISBN: 978-1-953196-27-9

Visit me at <u>melindacordell.com</u>

Gardens are not made by singing 'Oh, how beautiful,' and sitting in the shade. – Rudyard Kipling

Contents

PEST CONTROL FIXES

For squash, zucchini, or other garden plants afflicted by cutworms or borers, wrap a little aluminum foil around the plant's stem tightly enough to keep the pests out.

Add two tablespoons of light cooking oil to every gallon of organic insect spray. This will help suffocate aphids and other insect pests that are hit with this spray. Note: Don't spray oil mixes when it's over 90 degrees outside, as this adversely affects plants.

If you find slugs in your garden munching holes in your favorite plants, set out some saucers of beer for them. It might feel like you're rewarding the slugs for their bad behavior. Au contraire. The slugs get drunk and fall into the beer and drown. You might have to go outside twice a day and pick up the slugs that haven't drowned and toss them in a bucket of soapy water. Also, at the end of the day, you might dump the beer out so you don't invite hordes of drunken raccoons into your yard.

Japanese beetles can be knocked into a container of soapy water to kill them. Cover the Japanese beetles as they fall in because sometimes they fly away before they hit the water. If you have chickens, don't add soap to the water – just collect the beetles, then pour the water and beetles into their water dish for them to snap up.

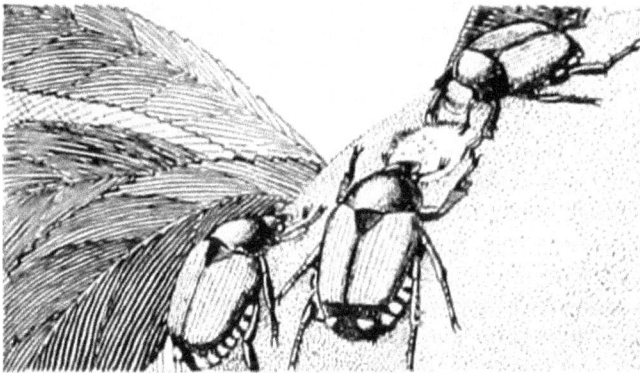

Deter slugs and snails by laying coffee grounds around your plants. You can also pour out the coffee you didn't drink around your soil. Snails and slugs avoid caffeinated soil, and a 1 to 2 percent caffeine solution will kill them. (Instant coffee contains .5 percent caffeine; brewed coffee contains more.) Slugs hit with caffeine fall to "uncoordinated writhing" before they perish.

A third way to get slugs and snails is with chalk. Chalk pictures drawn on the sidewalk make slugs explode. Grab your kid's sidewalk chalk, scribble all over a rock or a board, then put it under your hostas or cabbages where the slugs can crawl over it. Re-chalk everything each time it rains. Diatomaceous earth has the same effect on these and other critters.

Old milk, in a 50/50 mild/water blend, makes an effective fungicide for roses.

Charles Anctil, the late rosarian who I still miss, always sprayed his roses and plants with a blast of water from the hose to knock pests off the plants. It's an organic way to clean up insects, and it doesn't bother the plants.

If the cat keeps using your garden as a litter box, stick a bunch of plastic forks, tines up, in your garden. Or gather up a lot of pine cones and use them as mulch. The cats are not a fan of walking on pine cones.

If voles and mice keep devouring your flower bulbs

underground, you have several options. Surround each bulb with grit as you plant them, as rodents don't like digging through stones. Dig a trench, line it with chicken wire, lay the bulbs in it, wrap the chicken wire around them, then cover them with dirt. Or, place the bulb in a strawberry carton, place a second one on top, and plant them that way.

Have a kitchen shaker filled with diatomaceous earth. (Obviously, please do not leave this shaker in the kitchen.) Diatomaceous earth consists of millions of diatoms – microscopic, razor-edged remains of ancient sea organisms. Chalk is made of diatoms, which is why a chalk drawing will effectively kill a slug that slides across it. These diatoms cut through the slimy coat of slugs or the waxy coat of insects, causing them to dry out and die. At any rate, a kitchen shaker filled with DE can be shaken around hostas or other plants that are being attacked by pests, a nice and tidy way to distribute this pest killer.

Hang old CDs and DVDs in your fruit trees or strawberry patch to scare away birds and squirrels. Hang them so they dangle and twirl in the breeze. This also works with aluminum pie tins.

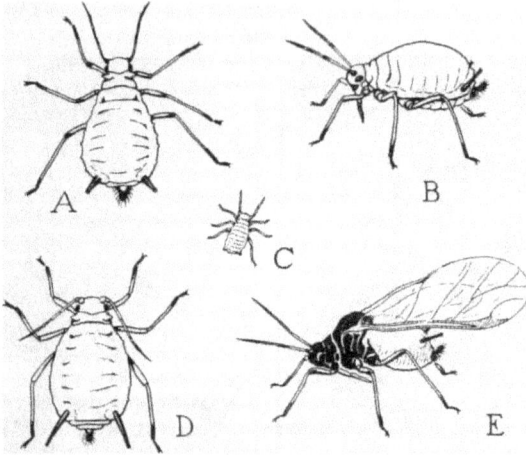

Five different forms of the same aphid.

Soft-bodied insects (aphids, caterpillars, etc.) can be cleaned up with soapy water pretty handily. I've had success in pouring a bucket of soapy water directly over the afflicted plant in cleaning up a number of these pests. The soapy water will need to be reapplied a few times to catch any pests that were hiding under a leaf or stem in the initial application.

On the other hand, birds are great pest control in the garden. One afternoon in the rose garden, I noticed a sparrow grabbing something off a rose with her bill and throwing it to the ground, and then she hopped down after it. It turned out to be a rose slug (i.e. a sawfly larvae), and she was picking them off the plant, throwing them down, then hopping down to eat them.

Set out bird baths for the birds to invite them into the garden to stay a while. Wren houses are also good to have (and I always love hearing the wrens singing when I go outside).

THE   EARLY   BIRD.

Getting the worm.

Put ripening fruit, such as apples and peaches, into zip lock bags and seal them around the stem as much as possible. This should help seal out bugs – and those damn squirrels!

Pinwheels in the garden help to deter critters! Just as long as your kids don't pick them all up and carry them away to play with.

Ant control in the house: mix 2 tablespoons Borax, 1 cup warm water, and a half-cup of sugar until it's dissolved. Dip cotton balls into the mixture, then set them in places that the ants frequent. They'll sip up the sugar water and carry it back to the nest to feed to the other ants. The Borax slowly builds up in the systems of the ants to kill them off – and this includes the queen ant, who lays all of the eggs. Once she's gone, that ant hill is history.

There's always the old "catch 'em in a barrel" trick.

An extreme solution to chasing off raccoons, rabbits, squirrels, etc.: Pee around your garden. Obviously, do this at night so the neighbors don't call the police. Animals take this kind of territory-marking very seriously and should leave your stuff alone. This isn't for the squeamish, but when raccoons keep getting into your sweet corn, sometimes you have to take strong measures!

If a pest infestation is particularly bad, cut the plant back drastically, then take the infested stems and leaves out of the garden to avoid re-infesting the plant. Then pour soapy water over what's left of the plant to get any exposed pests. The plant will come back, and should be in much better shape for it.

WATERING HACKS

Be sure to water plants while wearing the PUFFIEST SLEEVES IN THE UNIVERSE.

Fill an empty wine bottle with water, then place it upside-down (with no lid on it of course) in your flower pot. The water will slowly seep out and keep your plant roots moist.

You can also use a plastic water bottle, two-liter bottles, or a half-gallon milk or juice jug to help slow-water your plants. You can poke it full of holes, bury it in the soil (leaving the top of the jug sticking out just a little), and fill it with water, replenishing now and then when it starts running low.

For hanging baskets or any other planters that tend to quickly dry out, unfold a baby's diaper at the bottom of the basket before adding the soil and plants. The diaper is filled with water-absorbent crystals that will hold the water, and the layers of diaper will keep the water from running out all at once.

When putting plants in pots and containers, place a coffee filter at the bottom to let water run out and keep the soil inside the pot.

When you cook vegetables or macaroni, drain the water into a basin, and when it cools, use it to water the plants. Those nutrients that leached out of your food while it was cooking will benefit your plants as an organic fertilizer.

To keep mosquitoes and other insects from breeding in your birdbaths or water barrels, add a few drops of vegetable oil. The film that the oil makes on the surface won't bother the birds, but it will stop mosquitoes from laying eggs. Also, a teaspoon of liquid dish soap per gallon of water also does the trick.

SOIL BUILDING FIXES

Crush up your eggshells and sprinkle them on the soil around your plants. Better yet, dig them into the soil. They'll break down in the soil and give your plants calcium. If you dig them into the soil, the calcium is more available to roots. (Calcium doesn't move through the soil very fast, if I'm remembering this tidbit from Soils class correctly.)

Epsom salts added to your garden increases the nutrient absorption of plants and improves seed germination. A half-cup of Epsom salts, sprinkled around the base of your roses, encourage basal breaks in roses (which allows the rose to grow new canes) and decreases blossom-end rot in tomatoes.

Add used coffee grounds to acid-loving plants like raspberries, blueberries, camellias, hydrangeas, magnolias, roses, et cetera. Coffee grounds are rich in nitrogen, which causes lush, green leaves in plants and also encourages microorganism growth in the soil. Earthworms like them, too!

If you have chickens, fertilize different areas in your garden via chicken. Put up a temporary pen in your garden for a week or two, and let your chickens have the run of the place. (Put them up at night, of course, so raccoons don't start hanging around.) Then till and plant.

Trying to start a new garden in bad soil can be tough. One way to break up bad soil and add organic material is to plant large root crops. Potatoes are a good choice, as they have a lot of foliage to shade out weeds, and their tubers, if you leave them in the ground, add to the organic material when they rot.

Daikon radishes are also a good choice, breaking up soil

with their gigantic roots and adding organic material after the season is over if you leave them in the ground. (Of course you can pull up a few radishes and potatoes to eat.)

Alfalfa and red clover will send their roots deep into the soil, and both of these plants do a great job of fixing nitrogen into the soil. Alfalfa tends to turn woody, but its leaves contain a growth stimulant which can give your plants a boost in spring.

In winter, cover your garden with compost, throw a thick layer of organic mulch on top of it, and put earthworms in the soil, both nightcrawlers and red wrigglers. Let the worms do the work in the winter. By spring, you should be able to till the soil and have ground good enough to plant in. Keep adding compost and organic matter through the year to nourish the soil.

SEED STARTING TIPS

FLORISTS' FLOWER SEEDS.

A good way to make sure you have viable seeds is to pre-germinate them just before you plant them.

Soak large seeds like peas, beans, and corn overnight, then rinse and drain the seeds. Keep them wrapped in a damp paper towel for a few days until the seed coat splits and a tiny root appears. Plant these seeds at once, and water them in well.

However, if the legumes have a pink coating on them, don't soak them. The powder is an inoculant that helps the seeds germinate.

You can germinate small seeds by wrapping them in a damp paper towel, which you keep inside a plastic sandwich bag. Once the seeds sprout, plant the seeds into pots, one seed per pot, and let them grow in the house until the soil warms up and they can be planted outside.

Use old eggshells to start your seedlings, as these self-compost and add calcium to the soil as they break down.

Seedling containers can be made with all kinds of found containers. Egg cartons with holes poked in the bottoms, or clam-shaped plastic containers, work well, as well as yogurt containers and toilet paper tubes with the bottom folded up. Lemon or orange halves are also a possibility, though these won't work so well for plants that prefer alkaline soils.

Use toilet paper to make your own seed tapes. Roll out some toilet paper and mist it with water. Lay your seeds at the proper spacing all down the paper. Mist the paper again.

Fold a third of the paper over the seeds, then fold the other third over that. The seeds will be sealed inside. Then spray it again with water, let it dry, and roll it up on a toilet paper tube. You're ready to plant! When the soil is ready, unroll the strip, put the whole tape in the ground at the correct depth, and you're good to go.

Instead of using a heated mat to help germinate your seeds, place your seed trays on top of a refrigerator or on a table over a heat vent – someplace that already has heat.

Tiny seeds, such as radish seeds and lobelia seeds, are very hard to sow. George Ferbert, a local nursery and greenhouse owner for years and years, showed me this trick: Mix the seeds with sugar, then use a teacup or a salt shaker to sprinkle them over the vermiculite (a specific kind of potting soil used specifically for seeding trays). The sugar shows you where the seeds hit, so you can spread them evenly. An amazing fact: Lobelia seeds are even smaller than sugar crystals, if you can imagine that.

Plant two seeds in each pot. When the seedlings get big enough to compare, pinch out the smaller or the less husky seedling and let the bigger one take over.

Soak tomato seeds overnight in cooled chamomile tea before planting. The tea softens the seed coats, which helps germination. It also acts as a fungicide.

Damping off disease causes seedlings to keel over at the soil line and die. It's caused by a fungus, and if a patch of seedlings in a tray is affected, you usually have to throw the whole tray out.

To prevent damping-off disease, keep a small fan running over your seedlings to keep the air circulating.

If you change the pH of the soil's surface, you can make it harder for the fungus that causes damping off to get a foothold. Here are three easy ways to do just that and safeguard your seedlings against this disease:

1) Water the soil with cooled chamomile tea.
2) Sprinkle cinnamon on the soil, a light coating.
3) Sphagnum moss on the soil also works. I take dried sphagnum moss between my hands and rub them together over the seedling trays to cover them with this material.

These three things will help change the pH of the soil just enough so that the fungus spores that cause damping off can't survive.

INSTANT GREENHOUSES AND CLOCHES

Showing field set with
Hotkaps

Cut the bottoms out of two-liter bottles or milk jugs to make instant greenhouses for young plants in the garden. Take the lids off when the weather is sunny, and replace the lids when temperatures drop. Once the weather warms up and the little plants get husky, stack the bottles or milk jugs on each other and put them in the shed for next year.

Wash and save rotisserie chicken containers and clear salad containers to provide a small greenhouse for your new seedlings.

Row covers are lightweight cloths made for the garden to

cover plants. They are an excellent way to protect a lot of young plants early in the growing season, and they can also be used to protect root vegetables or cold-season lettuce and other leaf crops so you can grow them through the winter.

Row covers cost a little money. If you're a low-budget gardener, you can use a translucent tarp with holes in it, or an old white bed sheet.

You can bend chicken wire to make a tunnel that covers your rows of vegetables you want to protect, then lay the sheet, row cover, or tarp over it. Use binder clips to hold the row covers onto the frame to keep the covers from blowing off. Then fasten down the sheet on all sides, using boards or bricks, so the cold winds can't weasel in.

VEGETABLE GARDENING HACKS

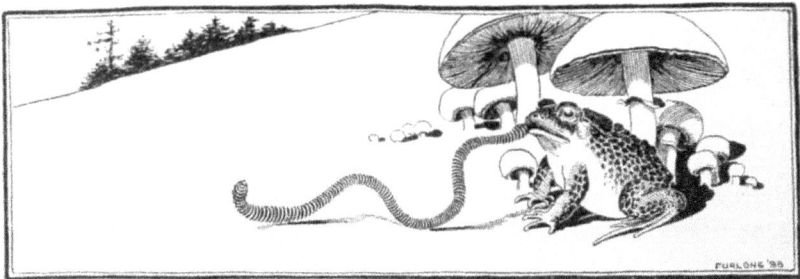

Are you impatient for the ground to warm up in early spring? Then lay a large sheet of black plastic over the garden for about a week, weighing it down with bricks, to speed up the process. Additional bonus: Weed seeds will start sprouting under the plastic. Move it aside, shear the weed seedlings off at ground level, then put the plastic back. When you're ready to plant, the ground will be warmed up and you've taken care of a number of early spring weeds as well.

In early spring, protect your young crops by placing a light row cover over them. This will keep pests like the cabbage butterfly and the rust fly from laying eggs on your plants. Also, the row cover helps keep your plants safe from sudden drops in temperature while you're at work or sleeping.

Plant marigolds throughout your garden if you've had problems with nematodes in the past. Midway through the season, the nematodes will take up residence in the roots. Pull the marigolds up and compost them (if your compost pile is a hot one) to get the nematodes out of the ground.

If you prefer your tomatoes to be a little sweeter or a little less acidic, sprinkle baking soda on the soil around the plants.

When the first frost is looming and you have a lot of green tomatoes, here's what you do. Wrap each tomato separately in brown paper and put them, stem side down, in a box. You can layer a piece of cardboard over each layer of tomatoes and then set another layer of wrapped tomatoes on top, clear to the top. Then store in a cool place. Take out the tomatoes as you need, them, ripen them in a paper bag with an apple for a few days, and you have fresh tomatoes.

If you have just a few green tomatoes to ripe, put them in a paper bag with an apple or with a banana. Those fruits release a gas called ethylene, which hastens the ripening process.

Or, you can just pull up the vines that the tomatoes are on, bring them inside, and hang them up in a warm, dry place and let them ripen that way.

Members of the mint family – spearmint, lemon balm, oregano, etc. – are notorious for sending out stolons and spreading all over the garden. If you want them in your garden, plant them in a plastic pot and then bury that in the ground, leaving an inch or two of pot above the ground as a barrier to the mints. Some places say to cut the bottom out of the pot – I'd just cut out part of the bottom, for drainage, but mostly as insurance against any out of control stolons that try to sneak out through the bottom.

Note: Oregano and chives (not a mint, but still a spreader) will reseed like crazy, so this hack won't be much help in that. However, if you can keep clipping back the plants to keep flowering at a minimum, and keep cultivating around the pot, you should be in decent shape.

Do you want to grow fruit but have a small yard? Try growing dwarf fruit trees. These stay very small – you can stand on a milk crate and reach most of the top branches – and they bear lots of fruit. One drawback is that squirrels can clean out the tree pretty quickly. Every time I'd look out my kitchen window in the fall, there'd be a damn squirrel hanging by its feet from the branches of my tree with an apple in its mouth.

This winter I picked up a wrist rocket with Nerf pellets that I'm longing to try on them. I also need to hang those CDs from the branches (this lifehack is in the first part of the book) to keep them out. They get plenty of corn from the chicken yard. You'd think that would be enough for them. But nooooo.

The squirrel mafia is up to their evil tricks again

You can also grow dwarf banana, pomegranate, lemon, and orange trees in pots, just as long as you have a warm place with lots of sunlight to bring them in to in winter.

When you're out of milk, fill the container with water, shake it up, then water your plants with it. They'll appreciate the extra nutrition it gives them.

Toss your tea leaves into the garden or into the compost – it all breaks down.

If you have a couple of cans of beer sitting around the house after a get-together, dump them around your plants in the garden. The beer actually acts as a mild fertilizer for your plants.

Squash bug hack: When it's squash bug season, keep a container of insecticidal soap ready to go nearby, with a little bit of vegetable oil added to it. Grab a water hose and spray water all over your squash plant and especially all over the ground. Then stop. After a minute, squash bugs will start climbing onto the upper leaves to get away from the moisture. Then you grab the insecticidal soap and spray them all.

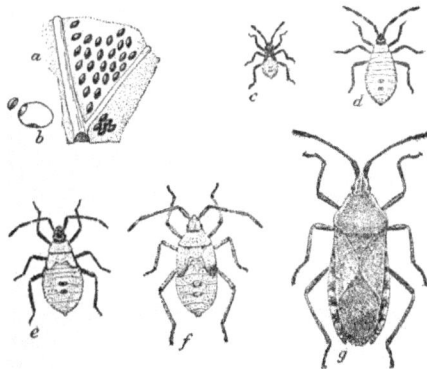

a. A raft of eggs tucked against leaf veins b. A vacated egg c., d., e., and f. nymphs in different instars g. Adult squash bug

CONTAINER GARDENING WINS

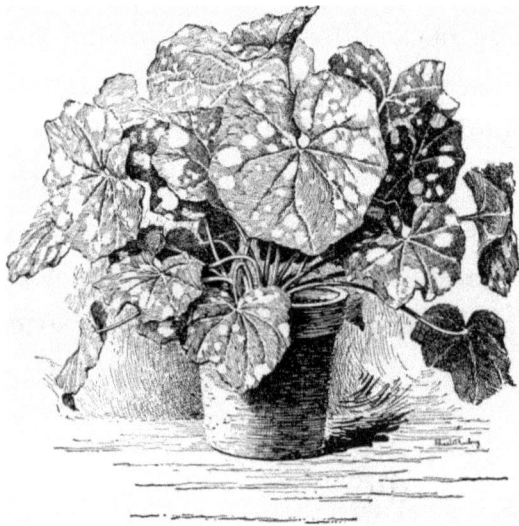

When you have a tiny yard, container gardening might be the way to go. Grow all your vegetable plants in containers. Choose determinate tomatoes, as they stay small and they don't take over the whole world.

Grow your potatoes in a half-barrel with drainage, or use a storage container with holes punched in the bottom. Plant your barrel potatoes in potting soil so you have a light soil to dig through. Then, if you need a few new potatoes to cook in the evening, you can plunge your hand into the soil and bring out what you need, and leave the rest to grow.

Do you have some old storage containers that are cracked or missing their lid? Use them to grow vegetables or flowers. Drill large holes, larger than the width of a pencil, in the bottom of the container. (Narrower holes don't allow water to drain.) Fill the bottom of the storage container with packing peanuts, or aluminum cans, or upside-down small pots, which keeps the container lighter and easier to move, and cover this with landscape fabric. Then put the potting mix in on top, and plant.

Garlic, leeks, shallots, and onions are great container plants. They don't have much in the way of insect or disease problems, and they don't need a deep container due to their shallow roots. The same goes for beets, radishes, and carrots. Probably not so much with Daikon radishes – unless you have a really deep container. In which case, go to town with them.

VERTICAL GARDENING WINS

Use gutters filled with potting soil as a way to grow plants if you are short on space.

Grow climbing beans on poles in the shape of a teepee so the kids can have a fort in the garden.

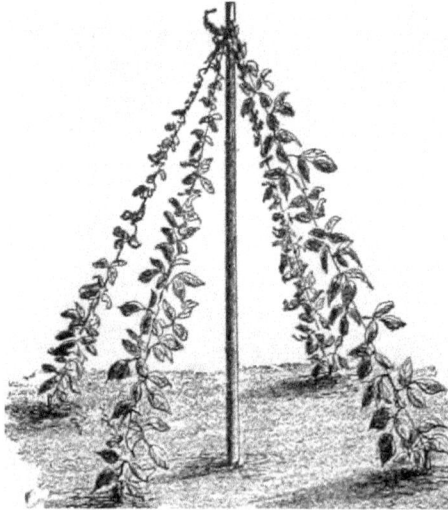

Use a PVC drain pipe with holes in it to grow strawberries vertically. Set it up on its end. Pour potting soil into it a little at a time, and have a friend there to help keep the dirt from falling out of the holes. Then plant one strawberry plant per hole.

Set up vining crops onto vertical fences or trellises. Send your squash, melons, and cucumbers growing up, not out. You can also do this with tomatoes.

If you're growing melons on a trellis, make slings out of old T-shirts to help support their weight so they don't break off the vine before they're ripe.

SETTING BEAN-POLES IN HOLES
MADE WITH A CROWBAR

HELPFUL COMPOSTING HACKS

No space for a compost pile? Put your kitchen scraps in an old fast food bag (a paper bag, of course) and bury them in the garden. Or bypass the bags altogether and put them straight into the soil near your plants.

Note: This might not work as well in sandy soils. I read about a gardener who moved to a place with sandy soil who tried to do some trench composting in this way in his new garden. Later when he tilled, all his produce came back up, just as fresh as when he buried it.

When you clean out your chicken coop in spring, put all the goods in your garden, or into your compost pile. Chicken leavings are high in nitrogen and other nutrients.

Use a blender. Drop in your kitchen scraps, add some water, and liquefy it. Then pour the slurry around your plants and water it in. Fast food for worms and plants.

Do you have friends who raise livestock? They'll give you free compost. They might even bring it out to you.

Direct composting in your raised beds is a way to raise

your earthworm population. Dig a hole in your garden, put in kitchen scraps, and cover it up. If you have possums or other critters digging in your garden for the scraps you buried, place a paving stone over the places where you've buried your scraps.

Tilleth thy soil with compost, good sir.

If your compost won't heat up and takes forever to break down, you might try composting with red wriggler worms. These are little red worms that you can buy at the bait shop. Put them in the pile and cover them with a little compost. They'll break down the compost and excrete worm castings, which is very mineral-rich and great for your soil.

If you have chickens or rabbits, put their manure in your compost pile. Manure is considered "green" materials – that is, they are high in nitrogen and will stimulate microorganisms in the soil like crazy. Add a corresponding amount of "brown" materials – that is, carbon-rich materials like dried leaves or grass, shredded newspaper, etc. When these brown and green materials are mixed in the correct proportions, the microorganisms that are stimulated by all that nitrogen are breaking down the green materials and also all the brown materials that are in their way. Then the pile gets hot – literally – for a while, and when everything settles down, all your raw materials are broken down and your finished compost smells pleasant, like soil. It's good stuff.

At the end of the season, spread your compost over the soil. (If you have chickens, let them help with this.) Then cover the compost with a thick layer of mulch, such as chopped-up leaves and straw. The earthworms will be hard at work all winter, digging that compost into your soil for you and leaving worm castings all over the place – black gold to plants. In spring, the work is already done for you.

Do you have a gardening space that needs improvement? Dig a hole in the ground there, layer in green and brown materials, and throw a layer of soil on top. Stop by occasionally to stir with a piece of rebar or chop it up with your spade. Keep the hole covered so you don't fall in. Throw in some more green and brown materials through the year and repeat. Then the next year, that spot is ready to plant in.

Sometimes you can get compostables from the local grocery store if you ask nicely. Or you can throw it to the chickens. You can get newspapers for your compost from the local convenience store or from your library. Shred the newspapers and mix them with your grass clippings.

MULTIFLORA BOUQUET ASTER

WEEDING TRICKS AND TIPS

To smother weeds over a large area, lay big sheets of cardboard over them. Large areas of old carpet will also do the trick, though you can't leave the carpet there permanently.

Cardboard or thick layers of newspaper to smother weeds, then build a raised garden bed right on top.

Newspaper mulch is an easy way to mulch the garden and quash weeds. Get a good stack of newspapers to start with. Unfold them and lay them, ten sheets thick, over the ground. You can even lay them on top of your weeds (stomp the big ones flat, or cut them down first). As you move across the garden, lay a second layer of mulch over the newspapers – grass clippings, wood chips – to hold the newspapers in place and keep them from blowing away. Then you have a nice, neat garden bed.

If a weed pops up, clear back the top layer of mulch, lay a thick layer of newspapers over the weed, then cover again with mulch. The newspaper mulch will smother out weeds.

Pillbugs, worms, and other small creatures will break the newspapers down into soil, breaking nutrients down for the plants as they do, but this work generally takes a full season or two – and by the time the newspaper mulch is broken down, the weeds have been smothered very handily.

If you're going to do a lot of weeding, or pruning, set a tarp out next to where you're working and throw the weeds on that. When you're done, pick up the corners of the tarp and drag them to the compost heap or your brush pile.

TOOL TIME TIPS

Fill a large clay pot with sand, and add mineral oil to the sand. When you're done gardening, you can put your small garden tools into the sand to clean, oil, and sharpen them all at the same time. Bonus: the oil will also protect them from rust.

To get rust off your garden shears, scissors, or pruners, use some very fine-grade sandpaper and gently rub the rust off. Crumpled aluminum foil also works. Then clean off the blade with an oiled rag.

lowland Long Handled .... 1 00 | English Rice Sickles, No. 2 .... 0'

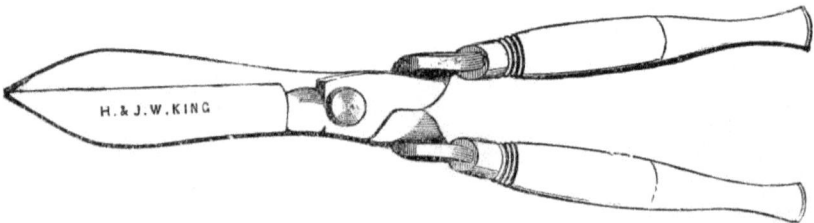

In winter, use a rag with linseed oil to rub down the wooden handles on the tools.

If you have an old mailbox, put it in your garden. Now

you have a dry place to keep your gloves, markers, small gardening tools, etc. And you can grow clematis on your mailbox, too.

Put some baby powder into your gardening gloves to make it easy to take them off after a hot, sweaty day.

Paint the handles of your gardening tools a bright color that shows up every time. Day-glo colors are especially easy to find among the raspberries.

If you don't have a wheelbarrow, use a sled to drag heavy items around the garden. You can also use a tarp or an old shower curtain for this task.

HOUSEPLANT HACKS

Use milk to shine houseplant leaves. Moisten a dishtowel or a paper towel with milk, then wipe the leaves clean.

Don't pour old coffee or tea down the drain. Water your plants with it. Coffee is a good source of nitrogen – this is good for green, lush growth. You can water acid-loving plants occasionally with coffee. With other plants, it's best to use it only a few times a month.

You can also water your houseplants, occasionally, with leftover beer. It's fine. They won't even drunk text you.

FLOWER GARDEN FIXES

When you have all your potted plants ready to go and you're ready to plant, check to see if your arrangement will work by setting each pot in the garden bed where you want it. Then you can see what looks right and what doesn't work, and switch things around, before you set them in the ground. I'd generally leave each pot where I wanted it as I was digging, or mark the spot each pot would go with a marker or flag.

Even when you are wearing leather gloves, roses are still going to jab you when you prune them. If you're fed up with this, use a clothespin to hold the rose while you prune them.

Use an old hair clip to attach dahlias, delphiniums, and tomatoes to your stakes. Make sure that the ends of the clips don't poke into the stem.

If you're trying out a plant or shrub that isn't quite hardy enough for your area, plant it in a south-facing area, perhaps with a brick or stone wall, or even a privacy fence, at its back. This creates a microclimate that stays a few degrees warmer than the area around it. Also, experiment with placing dark paving stones around the plant's feet in fall. These stones will absorb the sun and help keep the soil warm over its roots.

When digging a hole for trees, roses, or shrubs, lay a tarp next to where you're working. Throw all the dirt that you dig up on the tarp. Plant your tree, put the soil back, use all the extra soil to make a saucer around the tree to hold in the water, then dump all the dirt crumbs in the saucer, and fold up the tarp. The ground around the tree is just as tidy as it was before you started digging.

Roses love banana peels dug into the soil. The peels contain a number of minerals and nutrients that are good for these plants. They also love fish, so dig fish bones and fish parts into the soil. Then you'll have a fish tree! Just kidding. The fish is high in nitrogen, which roses love. Be sure to bury them deep, because animals also love fish.

FOOD PRESERVATION FIXES

Run your basil harvest through your food processor, then pour it into ice cube trays, top with a little olive oil, and freeze. Store the frozen cubes in a freezer bag once they're properly solidified (and write "basil" on the bag beforehand). Do this with each herb you harvest for that fresh-out-of-the-garden taste, even in the deepest part of winter.

Corn: Cut it off the cob into a bowl, add salt and sugar to taste, scoop them into freezer bags or containers, and pop the bags straight into the freezer. Fast and good.

Extra tomatoes? A quick way to deal with them is to drop them into a blender with a little basil, then puree them, pour them in a freezer bag, and pop them into a freezer. In winter, these are a great addition to your soup – just drop them in your soup pot and let them melt.

You can also put whole tomatoes into the freezer, freeze them, and store them in freezer bags until needed. When they thaw, the skins should slide right off. They are mushy, but if you're going to make them into soup or salsa, nobody will notice.

Raspberries, blueberries, strawberries, and other berries can be spread out on a tray. Then you put the tray into the deep freeze until they're frozen. Pour them into a freezer bag or container and they'll be good in winter.

The Cellar

LAWN LIFEHACKS

When mowing, don't bag your clippings. If you mow every week and the clippings are small, let them fall back into the grass. These clippings add nitrogen to the lawn and help fertilize the lawn.

Raise your mowing height, too. Taller grass can shade itself more, is more lush and thick, and makes a healthier lawn. Weed seeds have a harder time growing when the grass is tall and thick.

To keep grass from sticking to the mower blades, spray them with non-stick cooking oil. Silicone spray also works.

POND TIPS

If you have a small pond that keeps getting taken over by algae, use a garden rake or a hard rake (not a leaf rake) to rake the surface of the water and pull the algae and weeds out. Then put everything in your compost pile. Algae has all kinds of great nutrients, and especially trace minerals, that are a boon to your landlocked plants.

When you clean out your aquarium in the house, pour that water into the garden as well. The plants appreciate it.

When you catch insects or caterpillars in your garden, drop them into your pond for the fish. The fish should be happy to dispatch your pests.

When Japanese beetles invade the yard, knock them into

cups filled with water. Then give the beetles to your goldfish or your chickens. They will snap these beetles up fast.

MISCELLANEOUS HACKS

Add some salt to your soap when you have especially dirty hands that you can't get clean. This also helps remove dyes from your hands as well.

Use old pantyhose to tie plants to trellises.

Keep a small patch of wild area for local birds, critters, and insects. Many beneficial insects and birds need these spaces, and they do good things for your garden and for your area. Put up bird houses, bat boxes, and carpenter bee blocks.

Before you go out to garden, scratch a bar of soap with

your fingernails. When you come back in after grubbing in the soil and you wash your hands, you won't have so much dirt under your nails.

Start a co-op with your co-workers. Share your seed catalogs. Swap garden plants, trade eggs and zucchini and tomatoes, and share garden seeds. Show your friends how to harvest and preserve their food.

Our local library has a big seed swap every year. People bring in their extra garden seeds and leave with new varieties to try. There are some great folks at the Savannah, Missouri library, just so you know.

Or, if you have a harvest too big to handle, take some of it to the local food pantry. More than ever, people need all the help they can get.

If you have an old plastic mesh bag, put a couple of old slivers of soap in there and hang it next to the garden hose. Then you can wash up outside. The mesh bag is good for scrubbing off garden dirt.

GARDENING BOOK PREVIEW

DON'T THROW IN THE TROWEL: VEGETABLE GARDENING MONTH BY MONTH

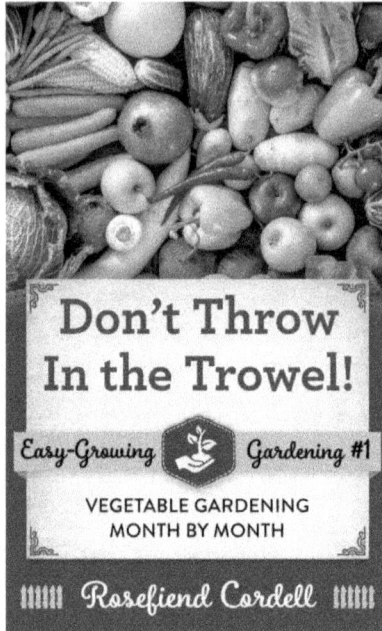

Even if you've never been a farmer or a gardener before, this vegetable gardening book covers everything you need to know to get started. Here you can find specific information about starting seeds, transplanting, mulching, organic fertilizers, dealing with pest and disease problems, compost, and of course, information about different vegetables and helpful advice on how to grow them. You can also find information about square foot gardening, beneficial insects (and insect pests), easy ways to keep weeds down, and ways to extent the growing season into the winter months using cold frames and floating row covers.

From *Don't Throw in the Trowel: Vegetable Gardening Month by Month*

JANUARY

Save Time and Trouble With Garden Journals

When I worked as a municipal horticulturist, I took care of twelve high-maintenance gardens, and a number of smaller ones, over I-don't-know-how-many square miles of city, plus several hundred small trees, an insane number of shrubs, a greenhouse, and whatever else the bosses threw at me. I had to find a way to keep organized besides waking up at 3 a.m. to make extensive lists. My solution: keep a garden journal.

Vegetable gardeners with an organized journal can take control of production and yields. Whether you have a large garden or a small organic farm, you must keep track of everything in order to beat the pests, make the most of your harvest, and keep track of spraying and fertilizing times.

Keeping a garden journal reduces stress because your overtaxed brain won't have to carry around all those lists. It saves time by keeping you focused. Writing sharpens the mind, helps it to retain more information, and opens your eyes to the world around you.

My journal is a small five-section notebook, college ruled, and I leave it open to the page I'm working on at the time. The only drawback with a spiral notebook is that after a season or two I have to thumb through a lot of pages to find an earlier comment. A small three-ring binder with five separators would do the trick, too. If you wish, you can take out pages at the end of each season and file them in a master notebook.

I keep two notebooks – one for ornamentals and one for vegetables. However, you might prefer to pile everything into one notebook. Do what feels comfortable to you.

Here are the five sections I divide my notebooks into – though you might use different classifications, or put them in different orders. Don't sweat it; this ain't brain surgery. Experiment a little. You'll eventually settle into the form that suits you best.

Good Quality S
5 in., 10c. each; $1.00 per doz.
7 in., 15c. each;

First section: To-do lists.

This is pretty self-explanatory: you write a list, you cross off almost everything on it, you make a new list.

When I worked as horticulturist, I did these lists monthly. I'd visit all the gardens I took care of. After looking at anything left unfinished on the previous month's list, and looking at the garden to see what else needed to be done, I made a new, comprehensive list.

Use one page of the to-do section for reminders of things you need to do next season. If it's summer, and you think of some chores you'll need to do this fall, make a FALL page and write them down. Doing this has saved me lots of headaches.

Second section: Reference lists.

These are lists that you'll refer back to on occasion.

For example, I'd keep a list of all the yews in the parks system that needed trimmed, a list of all gardens that needed weekly waterings, a list of all places that needed sprayed for bagworms, a list of all the roses that needed to be babied, etc.

I would also keep my running lists in this section, too – lists I keep adding to.

For instance, I kept a list of when different vegetables were ready for harvest – even vegetables I didn't grow, as my friends reported to me. Then when I made a plan for my veggie garden, I would look at the list to get an idea of when these plants finished up, and then I would figure out when I could take them out and put in a new crop. I also had a list of "seed-to-harvest" times, so I could give each crop enough wiggle room to make the harvest date before frost.

You can also keep a wish list – plants and vegetables you'd like to have in your garden.

Third section: Tracking progress.

This is a weekly (or, "whenever it occurs to me to write about it") section as well.

If you plant seeds in a greenhouse, keep track of what seeds you order, when you plant them, when they germinate, how many plants you transplant (and how many survive to maturity), and so forth.

When you finish up in the greenhouse, use these pages to look back and record your thoughts – "I will never again try to start vinca from seeds! Never!! Never!!!" Then you don't annoy yourself by forgetting and buying vinca seeds next year.

You can do the same thing when you move on to the vegetable

garden – what dates you tilled the ground, planted the seeds, when they germinated, and so forth. Make notes on yields and how everything tasted. "The yellow crooknecks were definitely not what I'd hoped for. Try yellow zucchini next year."

Be sure to write a vegetable garden overview at season's end, too. "Next year, for goodness' sake, get some 8-foot poles for the beans! Also, drive the poles deeper into the ground so they don't fall over during thunderstorms."

During the winter, you can look back on this section and see ways you can improve your yields and harvest ("The dehydrator worked great on the apples!"), and you can see which of your experiments worked.

Fourth section: Details of the natural world.

When keeping a journal, don't limit yourself to what's going on in your garden. Track events in the natural world, too. Write down when the poplars start shedding cotton or when the Queen's Anne Lace blooms.

You've heard old gardening maxims such as "plant corn when oak leaves are the size of a squirrel's ear," or "prune roses when the forsythia blooms." If the spring has been especially cold and everything's behind, you can rely on nature's cues instead of a calendar when planting or preventing disease outbreaks.

Also, by setting down specific events, you can look at the journal later and say, "Oh, I can expect little caterpillars to attack the indigo plant when the Johnson's Blue geranium is blooming." Then next year, when you notice the buds on your geraniums, you can seek out the caterpillar eggs and squish them before they hatch. An ounce of prevention, see?

When I read back over this section of the journal, patterns start to emerge. I noticed that Stargazer lilies bloom just as the major heat begins. This is no mere coincidence: It's happened for the last three years! So now when I see the large buds, I give the air conditioner a quick checkup.

Fifth section: Notes and comments.

This is more like the journal that most people think of as being a journal – here, you just talk about the garden, mull over how things are looking, or grouse about those supposedly blight-resistant tomatoes that decided to be contrary and get the blight.

I generally put a date on each entry, then ramble on about any old thing. You can write a description of the garden at sunset, sketch your peppers, or keep track of the habits of bugs you see crawling around in the plants. This ain't art; this is just fun stuff (which, in the end, yields great dividends).

Maybe you've been to a garden talk on the habits of Asian melons and you need a place to put your notes. Put them here!

This would be a good place to put garden plans, too. Years later I run into them again, see old mistakes I've made, and remember neat combinations that I haven't tried yet.

Get a calendar.

Then, when December comes, get next year's calendar and the gardening journal and sit down at the kitchen table. Using last year's notes, mark on the calendar events to watch out for -- when the tomatoes first ripen, when the summer heat starts to break, and when you expect certain insects to attack. In the upcoming year, you just look at the calendar and say, "Well, the squash bugs will be hatching soon," so you put on your garden gloves and start smashing the little rafts of red eggs on the plants.

A garden journal can be a fount of information, a source of memories, and most of all, a way to keep organized. Who thought a little spiral notebook could do so much?

Get *Don't Throw in the Trowel* today!

The author at five, with trowel and cosmos.

ABOUT THE AUTHOR

I've worked in most all aspects of horticulture – garden centers, wholesale greenhouses, as a landscape designer, and finally as city horticulturist, where I took care of 20+ gardens around the city. I live in northwest Missouri with my husband and kids, the best little family that ever walked the earth. In 2012, when I was hugely pregnant, I graduated from Hamline University with a master's of writing for children; three weeks later, I had a son. It was quite a time.

My first book, **Courageous Women of the Civil War: Soldiers, Spies, Medics, and More** was published by Chicago Review Press in August 2016. This is a series of profiles of women who fought or cared for the wounded during the Civil War.

I've been sending novels out to publishers and agents since 1995, and have racked up I don't know how many hundreds of rejections. I kept getting very close – but not close enough. Agents kept saying, "You're a very good writer, you have an excellent grasp of craft, but I just don't feel that 'spark'...." Even after *Courageous Women* was published, they still weren't interested in my books.

In September 2016, I rage-quit traditional publishing and started self-publishing, because I wanted to get my books out to people who *would* feel that 'spark.' In my first year, I published 15 books. This year I plan to repeat that. (When you've been writing novels for over 20 years, you're going to have a bit of a backlog.) I am working my way completely through it and having a complete blast. I love doing cover work and designing the book interiors. I work full-time as a proofreader, so I handle that in my books as well.

And now I'm finding fans of my books who do feel that 'spark.' They're peaches, every one of them.

I'm finally doing what I was put on this earth to do.

There's no better feeling than that.

If you like this book, please leave a review on my BookBub or Goodreads page. Reviews help me get more readers.

Thanks so much for reading!
melindacordell.com

Subscribe to my newsletter
and get a free gardening book!

www.ingramcontent.com/pod-product-compliance
Lightning Source LLC
Chambersburg PA
CBHW022106020426
42335CB00012B/851